MADLY IN LOVE

MADLY IN LOVE

POEMS BY

Aliki Barnstone

Carnegie Mellon University Press

Pittsburgh 1997

Acknowledgments

Some of these poems appeared in the following publications:

American Literary Review: "The Suicides," "Bright Snow," "Dream of Orchids" and "The Bath."
Berkeley Poetry Review: "Imperative."
Occident: "Heart Murmur."
Quarry West: Section 3 of "Night Unfixes the World" as "Night Rain."

Publication of this book is supported by a grant from the Pennsylvania Council on the Arts.

For their invaluable help with these poems many thanks to Tony Barnstone, Willis Barnstone, Beth Binhammer, Bruce Bond, Joseph Clark, Tim Fuller, Brenda Hillman, Andrea Musher, Lisa Rhoades, Harold Schweizer, and Nancy Sherman.

Library of Congress Catalog Card Number 96-83430
ISBN 0-88748-248-1

Printed and bound in the United States of America
10 9 8 7 6 5 4 3 2 1

for Joseph Clark

Contents

MADLY IN LOVE

MARCH WINDS

THE BATH

Then come to me now and free me
from fearful agony. Labor
for my mad heart,
and be my ally.

–Sappho

MADLY IN LOVE

Madly in Love

for Ruth Stone

Late one summer night he tore through
her latched screen door, his trousers
in his hand, and declared his love.
Then he lay down on the rug and screamed.
He was obliging when she asked him to leave,
and hiked from Goshen twenty miles
across the Brandon Gap in his underwear.
At six a.m., casually, as if he carried
a sack of breakfast bagels, he rang
our bell, trousers still in hand.
Three days later he committed himself.
He was a librarian, a sensible man.

As a child it mystified me.
Now I think despair could make *me*
walk twenty miles in my underwear.
I could lie down half-naked and wail
for an audience for my articulate loins.
I've screamed—haven't you?—even though
screaming means no one will listen.
And he was a librarian—I imagine him
knowing all the proper places for books
and for the lover in the stacks
who wasn't there when he clicked off
the fluorescent lights and drove

into mountains where the Milky Way's
silk sash billowed above him
and crickets sang out crazy excitement
as he stood on the dirt road with mountains
rising over him, wonderful, dark,
breathing desire. He saw her lighted
by a lamp and the fire, reading.
And for a moment, before he broke
through the obstructing screen,
liberating to the inside
mosquitoes and winking fireflies,
he thought she might respond.

After the Funeral

After the funeral we swam in the pool
of the beautiful apartment building
my uncle—he who chose to die—designed.

Every entrance was different, nothing
was identical and nothing could erase identity.
The copper edge-banding bled intentionally

into soft stucco, so fleshy and warm
against the bright Texas sky—and all reflected
in abundant windows and in the inviting pool,

the graceful, double-bellied pool,
Mexican-tiled, where we floated
or on whose edge we sat dangling

our feet into the water, parents and children,
aunts and uncles, nieces and nephews,
cousins and siblings, assuming our places

in the design which was not a design
but the accident of birth and of that unaccidental
death which assumed its place, too, and looked out

of the waters of this perfectly placed, perfectly
shaped pool where we laugh, search, talk,
or tell the story again of *why, how, if,*

and *but no it couldn't be helped*,
he was so sick but charming and a genius
and we loved him.

And again tell the story of what
came before and how inscrutably
we arrived at today,

each culpable, each susceptible,
now part of the design,
gathered here in his beautiful pool.

The Suicides

Even if I tell you the details of the funeral, the sentiments
of the eulogies, the moment I cried, that three white calla lilies

lolled their heads on the casket lid, that I let some earth fall
from my hand, then stood after the service with my family,

watching from a distance as a bulldozer finished the work
and filled in the grave, you must know the truth—

the suicides are never buried. The undead, they walk the face
of the earth not thanks to their uneasy souls but to make us

uneasy. My uncle slips into the passenger seat of my car,
recounting stories about us, planning a family event, analyzing

a design, telling a joke. I'm driving a Buick special, built
the year of my birth, laughing at his cleverness, glancing into

my rearview mirror, where I catch my grandfather grinning
at my cheek, wearing an elegant suit, a fedora from the 40s.

He opens the briefcase on his lap, holds up Swiss watches
and diamonds to the light. A magician, pulling eleven rings

from his sock and thumping his head to jostle gems
from his ears, his words are hummingbirds flitting

in the boxed air of the car—he's talking expansion to my uncle,
business is booming, they're so glad I'm going their way,

they say, giving directions, and won't I go straight into air
at the hairpin curve—drop to dream—into my red-blanketed bed,

the dark room, the snow-lighted windows where my insomniac eyes
blink at winter trees, those iced-over gashes on the night's skin.

Why must they sit at the foot of the bed, so interesting,
whispering family names with love? What's the secret question?

Who's next? Even if I tell you this and more, even if you
hold me now, if you want me and answer me, I hear their voices

in your kiss breathing, "It's only for a while." Nights,
nights like this when I'm chasing—what?—down a path

where there are no forks, the brambles are thick, dangerous,
closing in behind me, and I can't separate the roses

from the thorns, turn, stop, or go back. Do you see what I see?
Love goes away and tonight I'm invisible—even these words.

Psychology

I say I fear being healthy
in a sick world means being numb to it

(as if the window to a blue day were fogged
or bright blood were not like the poppy field,
not a shining red pool under spring sun).

And he says, Yes,
the woman whose husband's words

cut into her heart like swords
can make a shield against those sharp sentences,
can pick what to let in and what to close out.

The obsessive-compulsive whose meds free her
from ritual feels empty,

not knowing what to do if not worry.
So suffering is a habit, a choice.
And imagining my own death they call suicidal ideation.

And if I am a victim, passive, angry, tired,
dependent, hopeless, blue,

if my body and my mind hold hands
and conspire against me, I can change
the chemistry of my brain and talk it out.

My not sleeping three nights
won't save an innocent man from the electric chair,

won't do a thing
for the hungry, the poor, the tortured.
I never thought it would,

but I have reasons, losses, my desires thwarted,
and I could scream my fury

until the whole sky turned red,
as if all the gods of the past
slammed their fists through a mirror,

and the shards lay everywhere,
the fractured world making fantastic light.

And I have my pleasures which surprise me.
Even if empathy
is partially shit, sweat, and blood,

empathy is also making love,
the tongue in your ear,

a traveling, unpredictable sensation from which
(despite wisdom and toasting health
before a first intoxicating swallow)

I'm building silent utopias.
That must be why I laughed as I left the office.

His truth is undeniable and mine
persists invisible, a horrible wonderful something,
this self

flung against a wall, a stuttering voice.
This poem.

Heart Murmur

All this time I thought
it was the marriage,
that when hands inside me
gripped my guilty heart
I knew the origins
of the word *heartbreak.*
But now the doctor tells me
my pain is physical:
she hears a murmur,
a boom-shhha-boom
indicating
a mitral valve prolapse,
and drawing a diagram
explains the pain is not
the drama of psyche and soma,
but a valve ballooning
between the chambers of my heart.
Not degenerative disease
nor life-shortening,
I won't be
at risk in childbirth.
I've come through
those gasping minutes before
and I'll come through again.
And since it's congenital,
it was likely from my birth
I would feel pain
at this stage in my life;

and while the diagnosis
makes me fearful,
I see the pain
is without further consequence,
identified and constant.

With Skaters and Horses in Central Park

Someone falls. I'm looking for the artist. And while a few
skate backwards to the beat and glide with easy feet,

there is no spinning dancer, no beautiful lover of the ice.
The crowd holds hands in groups: some skate in a train, some

guide a novice friend. They look happy. It's the first Saturday
of the New Year and they're together, lovers and families.

I walk away over boulders whose crevices shine with bottle shards,
evidence of years of teenage passion and anger,

past a man, mesmerized, tossing cookies to the seagulls
diving over the unfrozen pond next Wollman Rink

where the crowd waits in line to skate in circles with the crowd,
back to the street and the line of carriages and horses,

the smell of horse, a bored driver in a top hat drinking coffee
from a styrofoam cup, tourists with blanketed knees, pointing

and talking. The last horse, a white one, waits, head down.
I hold out my hand for him to smell, run my fingers

along his enormous jaw and feel the sweet, soft fur of his nose.
He lifts his face away from me, then bows his head for more.

I palm the place between his eyes, stroke his muscular neck.
And again he sways away from me and toward me, as I leave,

turning back to see the horse slowly shifting from hoof to hoof,
his head rising and sinking, as if he were mimicking

my dance of vulnerability, longing, and resistance.

Night Unfixes the World

Doubt

You understand that night unfixes the world.
Sudden flappings out of the indigo sky
and doubts circle you like bats
sounding their way through houses and trees.
When you pull yourself from nightmares
it is useless to turn to the body next to you.
Motorcycles from the street below
tear at you like beasts you never see
yet know hover at your bedside
like a prayer for prayer.

Ocean

The ocean is a stranger you gave your body to.
Remember soothing surf,
breaths, your hair spreading its goldfish fins.
But your lover is whispering your name as a hex,
handling your belly, calling you flesh—
and you respond forgotten as you sink
pulling gold coins from behind your ear
as if performing for a child.
But each is stamped *Not True*
and you descend
to the animal's gold coin eyes
forgetting names like light, for like light
the waters' darkness undulates and grows.
Quick, think of something bright before your faith trips
and the ocean is a stranger who gave you its body.

Rain

Listen to the rain. It's wet but the sound singes.
You remember other rainy nights.
The million gray drops
were small horrified cries from a maze without walls.
You called a friend in a faraway place.
You took long hot showers to relax
and felt new rain on your skin.
That was long ago, yet sometimes you forget
the benevolence of water, the poppies and grasses
under the almond trees. You can't get dry or warm—
and then your confused senses
build fires at the back of your skull.
You listen to the rain; and for a few moments
every benign raindrop burns.

Ink

Drawing without a lamp as Twin Peaks darkens.
The cat coughs on its own hair.
You take pleasure in ink blots
leaking through the page like a thunderstorm
flashing over torn paper mountains. Ink tells you nothing,
is only other nights when traffic ticked
in your insomniac ear while your lover slept.
Is another period of argument.
And here you hiss the cat off the table,
shape this apartment, your face, headlight eyes
outside the window. Here traffic goes by
casting lights while blots of ink angels
silently travel the walls.

Bright Snow

Our winter is unimaginable
to those in other geographies.
The dailyness, the duration, the extremes.

First are preparation and work:
the miracle plastics stretched
with a hair-dryer across old drafty windows,

the corn cut down to stubble,
the bales of hay stacked up
to the farmhouse windows—

and the gardeners
prune precious roses hard
and make mounds of mulch

to protect their perennials.
Some bulbs must freeze to bloom,
but too deep a cold

leads other plants to death not rest.
Then come darkness and bitterness,
shrinking days, the solstice.

The melancholy landscape is everywhere
gray and heavy.
How could we humans have come

this far north, the wind
cracking down on us with a million needles?
No wonder our muscles contract.

No wonder we turn to each other,
each equally helpless when days are dayless.
Then at last, after the New Year,

comes the bright snow.
It snows all day and night
for three days and nights

and one morning we wake up to find
that snow is the sun's
cold but light-filled twin.

It's early.
Though the snowplow heaved by
and cast yellow spinning lights

for a moment on predawn bedroom walls,
the snow is mostly untouched,
and cars—unscraped and undug-out—

rise like a school of white whales
out of the ocean of snow.
Deep bright snow.

This is the illusion of payment:
that despair is a price paid
for the snow-covered field

being the sun's iridescent twin
and for each broken corn stalk
catching the afternoon sun

like a gold coin—
though that glow is nothing
but decaying stubble.

It's as ordinary as winter and work
and the voice that says
bright snow.

Beth Says She's Mourning the Passing of Winter

My friend Beth says she's mourning the passing of winter,
the months of white desolation
which are also freedom

and access to expanses
we can't traverse
in warmer months

when we stand on the lakeshore
throwing out fluorescent green tennis balls
for our dogs to swim after and happily retrieve

while those who own boats
own the waters.
But in winter we can all walk on water.

In spite of skiers, skaters, ice-sailors, ice-fishermen
and their lonely huts,
the frozen lakes are mostly empty,

and we walk far,
anywhere we want.
The snow says,

Shhh. Shhh. Shhh.
So we listen
to the enormous quiet.

Yesterday it thawed.
Today the temperature fell to two below zero
and with Beth I mourned the passing of winter

because the iced trees
made a web of light
in the blue morning.

Mist flooded the air
above the Yahara River
as its waters refroze.

I thought of the Chinese Song landscape painters
who practiced technique mechanically and painstakingly
to prepare for the moment

when passion would quickly guide them
—hand, brush, ink, and
eye—

to know where to leave
blank
so mist can sing its silence

to solid rocky peaks,
where to draw the smallest stick bridge
over a chasm

and the smallest meditating human soul crossing
into whiteness.
And

I thought the drunken Song poet-painters
        were like us,
                tiny companions walking together praising

a landscape brutally cold and bright
        that extends beyond our scope
                into thaw and loss

like the thousand frozen trees
        branching into seemingly infinite fractured
                light.

MARCH WINDS

March Winds

The snow is gone. Here and there one can spy
patches of ice. More often quiet green
pushes up in the fields where earlier a brief thaw
followed by a freeze glassed the snow

as if myriad ponds shone everywhere.
Damp winds blow off the lakes seeping through coats
and I'm impatient, chilled, taunted by odd warmths.
It's easy to be content with the dry zeros

that chap the skin, to be quiet indoors
or walk the frozen lake on a blue day,
watchful in a world sharp and contracted in ice,
where people slide in angular

light. Now tulips and irises poke green
butterknives through dark dirt. I sense
wisteria over my head, the scent, urgent
kisses, passion and dissatisfaction.

Dream of Orchids

> If we had a keen vision and feeling of all ordinary human life, it would be like hearing the grass grow and the squirrel's heart beat, and we should die of that roar which lies on the other side of silence.
> –George Eliot

Let me tell you about my orchids, I say,
showing a woman and a man into my house,

my sunny room, its wide window with orchids.
I've watered and fed my marvelous orchids,

have let them drain in the kitchen sink
before placing them back in the light.

I've protected them from winter drafts with a sheet of plastic
stretched to near perfect transparency.

I've waited through their dormancy
and have loved their sturdy, silent leaves.

And now they bloom and float in the air of the house,
soaring like rare birds

through some wildness,
through the crazed shifting light of tall trees' foliage—

like orioles drinking orange juice, heavenly bluebirds,
the wood duck with its red eye shining

as it drifts backward with the current,
or the great blue heron gliding, while under its gaze

were the Wisconsin River, sand bars, and mist,
and me whispering to my dog, "Hold still."

I take them in to show them my orchids,
a woman and a man in my sunny house.

"How lovely!" they say, admiring,
and I feel safe and warm,

a hothouse flower among hothouse flowers.
These blossoms last for months after months of nothing.

And they look like sex.
And they smell like the first day the ice breaks

when the neighbors are swing dancing in the park gazebo;
kids are shooting hoops—the ball sounds

like *poomf! poomf! poomf!* like a breath released,
like a love drug, like a memory freed from the clock

(whose sound is the smallest plot, since we say it says *tick-tock*)
so beautiful is everything moving.

But the woman is in my house,
breaking off the orchids' heads and leaving ragged stems.

She's pinned my orchids to her bosom,
as if they merely decorated a cheap prom dress

before the white-out of a camera flash.
Then she turns to the man for admiration.

And he takes her in his arms and wants her
to be one with him

and says there are no limits.
As I watch I can only watch.

I see her pin my orchids to her bosom
like the florist placing a corsage on a corpse.

Let me tell you about my orchids broken
in the sunny window, how they soared like rare birds

and would have bloomed for months after months of nothing
and smelled like sex

and felt like the rushing sound of ice flows,
like the silence in which we hear the voices of bodies.

They looked like the smooth skin of sex,
felt like breath quickening when love's exposed.

And how I raged when she turned to him,
wearing my broken orchids,

and I saw she was me.

What Takes Place

is the drama of winter letting go,
giving way to stinging color,
like the prisoner released,
shading her eyes from the sun.

All day the landscape: gold fields
vanquished by noisy green,
the convolutions of apple orchards
and huge weeping willows.

My task is to give you up,
but just as I begin to let go,
hopelessness flowers:
a boy is in your place, your past—

not you, but someone I loved before
you, who like you seems
one way and ends up another.
He says you'll be back. You will

come back, like the others, not to me,
but in me, just as these bare branches
circling in impassive sky
will erupt at once.

Today I watch baseball practice,
T-shirted boys tossing balls
on a playing field where a strip of snow
still clings to the earth near cool trees.

Wanting to see solely that pure scene,
I gauge how much time
it will take until spring takes you
and takes your brothers.

Imperative

The men are dead. Yes, and the boys are dead too.
Let's take them in our arms and weep
because they are cold and unreachable.
Let's kick the dirt gleefully into their graves
because they are cold and unresponsive.
Let's go home and pound the walls
because our beds are empty
and we didn't get what we wanted.
Let's rock numbly in our chairs blaming ourselves
because we chose it
and we got exactly what we wanted.
Let's raise them from the dead,
let's kiss the breath back into them and tease
their penises erect. Let's do it before we die.
Let's fill their minds with glory and possibility
and take them inside us and let them
fill us with glory and possibility.
Let's say, let's do it again.
Let's examine our histories and bury the dead,
resurrect them and kiss them again and again.
Let's hope. Let's take them in our arms and weep.

Fairy Tale

Before the good prince takes the good maid away
the fairy casts a spell on the evil sisters.

Each time they speak, lizards and snakes and toads
fall hissing from their mouths, as if the body

held in all bad and all the bad were released
embodied. Now since we're undressed for love

and love's a hard word, a lump in our throats,
a woman appears casting spells with her hands.

Her touch is awful, hurts, is good. Something
unspeakable she forces from our bodies.

It's worse than dirty. Not urine or feces
or what we know of sickness and of health.

It must be venom in all its consistencies,
the human secretions of anger, turning toward

and away, touch withheld, resentment, the child
happy and unafraid then ashamed and sulking.

Afterward you'd think we'd be cleansed. We have
a moment of quiet, hope, a kiss. But before

we're good again. I must be like the girl
who knit the sweater of nettles and then wore it,

who sucked three iron loaves down to nothing
while walking barefoot through desert and winter.

I'll live in three houses, and love and lose
each one. I must have three hateful husbands:

one who bores me, one who won't let me out
of his sight, one who beats me. Then I'll be free

to kiss you again. Then I'll wake from this dream
just as I did this morning. Spring light warmed

the sheets, my skin—so I wanted to make love
in the sun. But you would not hear my words

or feel my touch. I saw my evil sisters—
and all around me, hateful slithering things.

Oh, No!

I go into overdrive,
want to do just one thing lucidly.
Maybe smash all twelve wine glasses I got
at a yard sale—a screaming deal—

bang my head against the door.
The car goes, *Drive fast!*
I'm shouting, *I hate you and love you*
and hate you and I love you!

Then I see my drama
as so much action,
oversimplified,
a sky in the box labeled sky,

dirt in dirt, shit in shit,
and so on. And my position,
disembodied, closed, lacks colors.
The same stranger repeats, *Hello!*

on the other end of the line,
wrong number by design.
Better to go slowly
and think about friends.

Be a sleepy dog
looking up affectionately.
Watch the Giants on the tube.
All this urgency

makes me lose sight even of a string
I nervously wind around my fingers,
then feel fall away from my skin,
or of something I saw in many places

and in many lights,
or couldn't see at all.
All night I do this, absently,
talking to you as if it amused me.

Prescription

When I come downstairs after my shower,
she says, "You look like a waif."
And it's true my navy blue pajamas
hang from my burdened shoulders.
I'm thin and overwhelmed by the bath towel
on my head. I say, "So do you,"
and hug her and feel her rib cage small
and her shoulder blades stark, bony,
like the stumps of amputated wings.
I joke— "I have never seen a vision!"—

quoting from the true-false personality test
that led to diagnosis: depressed.
So we take a pill a day to drive
the blues away, can't eat and are thin,
good girls, admired, compliant.
She's grieving and I'm angry.
I'm grieving and she's angry.
Never mind, our feelings flew away
with our wings, our sexuality,
with a perceiving sense of touch

(of just how this plastic keyboard feels
now under my fingertips) and that self
attuned to the expressions of the sky—
heavy gray, mysterious black, or exalted blue.
We're so good we can't swallow, but the bad
races in the bedroom windows by nightfall,

inserting itself. And if we wake screaming,
if we sleep where the house is bombed,
family dies, and someone nightly burns
our books and papers, still we wake numb

until we say no, and over a slow month
the chemicals drain out while it all returns
like a flock of honking Canada geese,
just as silly and grand.
"I wanted to feel," I say.
"They don't tell you," she says.
They sit like gurus in their altar of texts.
"It seems you're depressed," they say,
consulting a notepad.
And I've just begun to be bad,

to feel spring bloom in my loins,
each budding oak, the lilacs shining with the lakes.
And I can long to feel someone's skin
as profoundly as I feel my own,
now when I'm naked in warm-cool spring air.
I can spit out hatred for the prescribers
as surely as I've been cooking up
this poem for a long time and today
I sit at my feast and enjoy every bite.

Argument

I escape out onto the front porch swing.
Through windows of apartments across the street,

I see the inner walls where dramas play
in lightning and flickering, those urgent

shifts of scene and coy narrative winks,
the TV programs numb eyes watch. Ubiquitous evil,

I think, then revise (no, just a common seduction)
feeling now what is *now* is

a science fiction society which I imagine
as if I were apart from it.

I kick the porch rail, sail
back toward the house—forward toward the lake.

Of course—I pray—retreat—and rage—grieve.
Gimme a break. If I weren't disoriented—

so damn dizzy—I'd stamp my foot and cry,
Why keep rehearsing this dumb drama?

I don't even want to talk about it.
I jump from the swing, leaving it swinging,

and stomp my feet down stairs to the lake shore
where I spiral inward to *I, I, I,*

outward to the night
and the lake coiling under the waning moon,

a wide-spanning bowl tilted in air,
pouring its light into numb waters.

But fuck it. These waters are still dark
with my smart misery.

Moon

Who in her right mind talks to the moon? I do.
I have looked to the moon to pray: let someone far away

look with me toward your face. That's what lovers do
whose faith is strong. But doubt is trees, parked cars,

and still houses rendered shadows (even under the full moon)
whose shapes I fill in, while I sever the whole

neighborhood (where I live) from the light-cut lake
mirroring the moon's solitary look.

Tonight I make my request: help me with this loss.
And the moon steadily fills the dark with itself,

its face open-mouthed as if, calling out in suffering
long ago, its expression remained fixed and its light

kept changing, as tonight its familiar visage plays
on the waters of the lake and brightens the summer

ripples moving in a slight breeze and humid heat—
such quickness and such heaviness—blades of white

shifting against each other like a fast-handed crowd
sharpening knives, and like my mind slicing away excess

to reveal a lightened center.

For Buck

When we leave, Buck chases the car
for miles out of town. Then brought home

again, howls a dirge all night.
Who can say the dogs don't suffer loss?

I think they mourn with absolute purity,
with no words to form a memory, consolation

or hope of return.
Today what we assume confuses me,

the faith that each leave-taking is temporary.
The dog yelps out his happiness

each time he sees us, and now our scents
still linger in the carpet where he lies,

but we're not there—no hands in his fur,
no voices saying his name. And so at night

he urgently goes to each house we took him to,
searching for the ghostly human friends.

Ending

The rain has stopped and I stand in our yard
in my bare feet though the stones are cold.
The young trees we planted release tiny leaves
in their first spring—the crab apple, the stand of birches,
the two apples, two cherries, two pears, the red maple.

So too have the early spring flowers begun to bloom:
daffodils, tulips, Dutchman's britches, flox,
grape hyacinths, bleeding heart, and bloodroot,
whose flowers, chaste white spheres, close-petaled,
bloom close to the ground and to their red, staining roots.

Perennials are a strange faith—what's nurtured
and loved, protected from cold and disease, endures
as if order were beautiful, redeems our hope
and the measure of joy with which we chose our plants,
then waited for the colors they make in their freedom.

Soon this will not be mine. It's dark, what's called
the wee hours—and so they seem too short to me.
The rain drops peep with the night birds and insects
and with the train baying to warn of its own passing
Into silence and nothing, I think. Then correct myself,
since a train goes to the city named your destination

and it is merely me who hears a short-lived cry extinguished
and feels Midwestern cut limestone, a garden path,
the work of love, the soles of my feet on cold, wet stones . . .

THE BATH

The Bath

I'm taking a bath thirty-six years, seven months,
and three days after my birth.

Outside I hear the city of Madison hum out
its dumb question, *Hu-u-uh?* One long, constant note.

No sirens or screams, no tornado warning, no people
laughing on the street because it's spring, nothing like that.

Inside the bathwater clicks or plinks,
clearing its throat or breathing regularly,

saying *please, please, please, please, please,*
ditto, and ditto again, like that, under its breath,

so you just make out its loneliness. I hear these things
because I'm asking, *Am I inside my body? Am I a work of art?*

and prop myself up, so one calf and ankle and foot,
then the other, float. So one forearm and wrist and hand,

then the other, float. Skin in warm water is rosy.
Breasts float like water lilies.

I am a woman who's not given birth, soaking the tension
out of my back, alone in the bath, seeing if I can

objectify myself while my heart goes out to some you,
out through the fogged window, sighing like the body

of water—warm, elusive—out over the dumb groan of city
and the slushy, melting lakes streaked with those signs

of both solitude and society: lights of streets, windows, cars.
This is not what we call longing, yearning, desire, horniness.

This is not a memory of someone who admired my breasts
or with touch transported me inside myself.

Can you imagine something else? Not the image of lovers
in the mind of a woman alone in the bath, speaking to the

blankness of bathroom walls or the blankness of the page.
Imagine now I can't see my face, only these floating hands,

heels hooked on the bathtub's rim, these strange, weighted
limbs, unfamiliar a moment, though little changed in years,

as if I were newborn and had no words and no past,
no way to identify this—this what?—this thing lying in water,

trying to unwind, a little bitter to be alone in her body,
questioning, pleading, trying to please, and unable to exit

her conversation with you or the pleasure of these words
forming out of water, the pleasure of being in the bath.

Ocean Fruit Stands

Nancy cried out, "The clarity of Cal!"
when the mist burned off the Brussels sprouts fields
and the air cleared where big waves broke

high as the cliffs, as if sky were a blue pitcher
pouring its turbulent twin into the ocean.
Gulls materialized out of the white crash

and sandpipers raced from foam toward us and away.
I said, "The sea lions are singing our song,
mournful and sexy. These years I haven't seen you,

I've come here when I'm down.
When you see a fountain burst out there
in placid water, it's a whale."

California poppies bloomed everywhere
out of dryness and stone, little flames
of hope. Then she cried out again,

"The boats on the bay!"
Strawberries the size of a child's fist,
sweet, juicy, staining our fingers pink.

Artichokes at the roadside green-grocers'
ten for a dollar; kiwis the same.
As we drove home, strawberry aroma

mixed with the ocean air rushing in
open windows. "These are benevolent
fruits and vegetables," I said,

standing in the sunny kitchen, cooking
artichokes with egg and lemon sauce,
fruit salad, raw, fresh greens decorated

with the hot spice of nasturtium petals.
We ate under the confused lemon tree,
its blossoms, white, waxy, inebriating,

its thin-skinned fruit already ripe—
"It doesn't know if it's spring or fall,"
Nancy said. "So it's giving its all."

"It never gets too cold here," I said.
Lifting our forks slowly, we shared artichokes,
strawberries, kiwis, antidotes for despair.

Solstice

Dogs howl with the wind, no one knows why.
I say they know what they know, just as I know
the season of summer storms means a thrill.

The stillness deepens just before the sky turns green,
makes the streets green rivers. Alarms and radio
electrify the city with warnings to take shelter.

On the plains, winds spin out tornados
and dogs howl out love, and we howl with the dogs.
We play piano, guitars, spoons, bongos, kazoo,

slapping our thighs red, while the storm thunders
—ardent, wet, bright, thrashing—
its humid air mixing with our sweat.

Hands flourish all around me,
and I dance as if I could stand it alone
another light summer hour.

The Friend of the Body

It is the small creature that moves inside the body,
fills the lungs with cool raw light,
slides down the spine, and undulates in the pelvis.

You must lure it from hiding, though it coaxes
you with a kiss. You kiss my back and it
understands the back of the body is what cannot

be seen, just felt. Still when we love it asks:
"What word is this?" It wants your stories,
wants to tell you mine. All nerves, the creature

knows it bears the wounds but cannot bear them,
shrinks into the heart where it can neither stay
nor leave. In these private chambers

you will find the creature waiting for you, its friend.

A Beautiful Day

Let me stand here. And let me pretend I see all this. . .
–C.P. Cavafy

Transient clouds sail in clarity
and the trace of moon floats suspended between

day and night, as if by parachute, as if
I could stop here and look longer than I can

at so much loveliness, perfect light
moving quickly, varying these myriad colors,

contrary light moving fast yet in slow-motion caresses.
Let me pretend I can see all this

without blurring the beauty with loss,
that I am saved mid-fall and drift with the wind chimes

and all at once—so much singing!—when sparrows,
swallows, robins, blue jays, fluting cardinals

soar from tree to tree, bird-multitudes, wings
beating out their wild time and mine, too.

Let me practice idiot glee—Nothing is still!—
and I could hold in me this beautiful changing

and changing day through any misery.

A Humid Summer Day

How humid it is today, the sparrows darting
in and out of tall trees.
Why can't I love you as I love what we made?

The heaviness of hands, the lightness of hands.

I overlook the garden I shared creating.
Oriental lilies, ferns, cosmos, and daisies revel in moisture;
hostas spread wide wings over black earth;
vegetables wait for harvest.

The cardinal's whistle sears the sky.

But heat and wetness, so beneficial to plants,
are restraining hands on my head.
Heavy hands, light hands.

Herbs and roses scent the air.

I love you is a spell cast by poems, TV, radio songs,
by summer and its trance of bounty: long days of light
and sleeplessness,

the spreading verdure of the land,
the sky glazing green before unleashing storm,
tornadoes, rivers flooding their banks,

agitated dreams, desire.

The heaviness of hands, the lightness of hands.

Summer in the earth and in the sky acts out its abundance
while I speak out scarcity:

I'll leave you with the hindsight
of the blankness on the other side of plenty,

vast blank fields of snow—

all the possibilities following this
blank page.

So This Is Grief

The day I see the first winter light, the professor
in his worn suede jacket stands in the parking lot
while a few still yellow leaves

blow wearily about. His face is gray like the sky
and the students walk to class, sick of the routine.
So this is grief.

Three hyacinth glasses gleam in the dishrack,
tinged with green, ready for me to fool bulbs into belief
that it's spring.

And the bulbs wintering in the refrigerator
lean their purple skins against the cider.
The way it is with me, words can't help.

Now that we're estranged—strange word—for good,
analysis doesn't matter. How might it feel
to go back again and pass the house

I no longer own where strangers hang their coats
in the vestibule? They'll sink into an easy chair
on a day so cold the keys stick in the doors.

They'll live in the living room, and will they notice
the frozen lake I focused into a hardness of thought,
a moment slicked over like the first day of solid ice?

I could walk as far as I wanted there, feet passing
over the lake's lens amplifying weeds and depths.
It did no good to talk about what we saw.

So this is grief. You have red hair.

Downriver

Before dawn I left the small town,
its sleeping-standing-up church steeples,
its three-globed street lamps lighting the bridge.
There below the rooftops,

I crossed the twice-mown lawns,
and my black dog took her joy to the river.
How placid its surface!—
the currents' force barely visible.

The fleeing spirit of the night turned gray,
while water and early sun like lovers
undulated together. I had to swim,
for floating is my first happiness,

and let myself in the water,
giving myself to pleasure,
the water's fingers touching
all my skin with perfect pressure.

Then the current embraced me
in awful arms. I thrashed
and called out to my dog,
whose grim face bobbed just out of reach.

I wondered, how long could I tread water
without getting cold, and would we drown?
The town slunk off, as if to turn aside.
The river hurled us away from the banks

but it never pulled us under,
and took us close to its center.
As I spun slowly in the water's hands,
I lost my fear of what came before.

Then, my dog running close beside me,
I clambered up the banks of dream, and lay alone
in bed, and trusted I would not drown.
Now who would float against me with slippery skin?

Love Poem

Because it is a winter morning, the light plays silver
with my hand on your chest and the lost child slips in
between the coats hanging from the door hooks.

Music is you speaking or singing who knows what in the shower,
a trancy guitar, a murmuring voice, wind and rain
against freezing windowpanes, incomprehensible syllables

I love and want to hear since something's taking shape,
this one and that one and the one I was, gone a decade ago,
traveling West while you traveled ever further East.

So we meet here.
(*Breaking a taboo, I show you this, incomplete.*)
Words come the way

I slip into my wetness, where you were, in the dreamwave
where the ocean and the sun converse, waiting to catch
the high one, the one I ride in turbulence—

with saltwater flushed eyes and sand scoured skin—
to your shore, to—how improbable—I knew you
before I knew you.

Not that the Lord ensconced at a mahogany desk,
pulling his vast beard with a ubiquitous frown,
determined our fates.

Not like the hostess, touching our arms, her heat palpable,
"It's perfect. You're made for each other."
The dog climbs in the bathtub, looks out

from behind the shower curtain, wagging her tail.
"What are you doing in there?" Silly. I talk to dogs.
They are better than Beings—because they know—but do
not tell.

You go with me to the field where yellow gathers in one spot,
warming an immense boulder. I curve my back around the earth,
arms outstretched, feeling it turn—

I could not hope
to touch the sky
with my two arms—

yet I feel your being breathing where I breathe, understanding
when you're a child, your feelings don't lie . . .
when the green woods laugh with the voice of joy,

when the painted birds laugh in the shade.
We laughed beneath the forsythia thumbing its nose at the sun
and beneath roomy coats in the closet

that smelled of gardenia,
and of the tiny bells pinched from lilies of the valley,
of the lives of dead relatives and the stories

we made up out of their belongings, of dirt we dug
with sticks and fingers, and of the sweat wet under our knees
as we squatted there, showing ours.

And he said, Who told thee that thou wast naked?

You get your face slapped for too much joy,
for lacking judgment about what feels good,
for loving as if fucking full of bliss were

the only meaning, all that matters.

Suddenly, I am stammering in the face of Probability,

though I have my own proof. Before we met I studied
all night to avoid the others. When the birds sang and
light was a narrow ridge between still dark mountains and sky,

I briefly slept. I got up for class. Afternoons I left them
again to sleep, again to dream you into being. I wrote,
In this room is the man I meet only in dreams.

I come to him always in cities I've never seen.
His eyes are the unnatural cobalt of heaven.
His teeth are a leaf from the tree of lights. His lips.

He knows what I am thinking. Remember that line of thought?
Haven't we met before? Oldest line in the book.
We weren't ready then, seeing so much beauty but blind.

It lay unmentioned—and now it's cast up from childhood:

Pearl and Weed, something repels you yet you love.
Passion. Passion!—Write it twice. It's so much it wants
the whole blank page and the blank page wants you,

steadfast, happy in your freedom, wants the vast
—the coil of love in a small room—
and wants something sweet—snow on the tongue,

paragraphs invented by a hot bath,
or a city-world drawn in a matchbook,
wants dailyness, waking as spoons,

and remembers you ordering an omelette,
the serendipity of a cut yellow rose
glowing under your chin, a homely table,

you saying you love me with passion, not cupidity.
Perhaps Affection has always one question more
which it forgot to ask.

This morning I show you these incomplete words.
"Give the child a voice, too," you suggest,
"What's she saying from between the coats?"

"I don't write like you," I retort, though I'm hearing
the music, *vital things that wake to bring*
news of birds and blossoming combined

with your sitting here, simply, in a chair.
You joke, "You think I'm being solipsistic,
but I still hold myself against you." And you hold me

as the lost child slips in and out of our conversation,
and the light plays silver with hands on hands
—on morning-wingéd feet whose bright print is gleaming—

on some word mumbled inside the self
as I hold you to me,
continuing.

Notes

EPIGRAPH These four epigraphic lines are the last stanza of Sappho's "To Aphrodite," translated by Willis Barnstone.

ARGUMENT /40 *Of course—I pray* and *Smart misery* are derived from Emily Dickinson's poem #376.

LOVE POEM /60 *They are better than Beings—because they know—but do not tell.* –Emily Dickinson.

I could not hope / to touch the sky / with my two arms. –Sappho.

when you're a child, your feelings don't lie. –Rick Bass.

when the green woods laugh with the voice of joy, / when the painted birds laugh in the shade. –William Blake.

And he said, Who told thee that thou wast naked? –Genesis.

Suddenly, I am stammering in the face of Probability. –Lucie Brock-Broido.

It lay unmentioned— –Emily Dickinson.

Pearl and Weed. –Emily Dickinson.

Perhaps Affection has always one question more which it forgot to ask –Emily Dickinson.

vital things that wake to bring / news of birds and blossoming. –Percy Bysshe Shelley

morning-wingéd feet whose bright print is gleaming. –Percy Bysshe Shelley.

About the Author

Aliki Barnstone was educated at Brown University (B.A. and M.A.) and at University of California, Berkeley (Ph.D.). Her volume of poems, *The Real Tin Flower,* introduced by Anne Sexton (Macmillan), was published when she was twelve years old. Her poems have appeared in *Poetry, New Letters, The New York Times, Ms., Agni, Chicago Review, The Antioch Review,* and other journals, and she is co-editor of the anthology *A Book of Women Poets from Antiquity to Now* (Schocken / Random House). At present she is editing the forthcoming *Voices of Light: Women's Spiritual Poetry from Around the World* (Shambhala). Aliki Barnstone lived and went to school in Spain and Greece and has traveled extensively in Guatemala, China, Tibet, and Burma. She teaches at Bucknell University.